That's nothing!

RODERICK HUNT

Pictures by Chris Smedley

Oxford University Press

'I don't want to brag.
But my mum
can climb any mountain crag,
put up a flag,
and parachute down
in a paper bag!'

MUM

'That's nothing!'
'How's this for a thrill?
My mum can ski downhill
with a tray of soup,
circle the group,
stop – and not spill a drop.
I call that skill.'

‘That’s nothing!’
‘That was just luck.
My mum’s got pluck.
She doesn’t mess about.
Once, she saw a ten-tonne truck,
stuck! It was in some muck,
so she just pulled it out.’

H H
10 TONNES
HARRY'S HAULAGE
BIG LOADS
HH

MUM'S DRUM

'That's nothing!'
'Listen, chum! With my mum,
anything goes.
She can play a drum,
blow a trumpet and hum,
strum a guitar,
and play a harp with her toes.'

‘That’s nothing!’
‘I don’t want to crow,
or show off, you know.
But my mum has a great wrestling throw.
She can throw any man
into the second row,
my mum can.’

FIRE
EXTINGUISHER

'That's nothing!'
'Do anything, my mum will.
Once, when her neighbour Bill
was using his grill,
he set fire to his flat.
Mum jumped over the window sill,
put out the fire – and that was that!'

'That's funny!
My mum's late,
it must be the weather.'
'Mine's late too.
Let's go to the gate
together.'

'Mine's not here yet,
I wish she'd hurry.'
SCHOOL
'When mine's late,
it makes me worry.'

'My mum lost her keys,
you know what mums are like.'
'That's nothing!
My mum had a puncture on her bike!'